Teach Yourself

SNOOKER

Rachna Jain

B.A., LL.B.

SPORTS PUBLICATION

7/26, Ground Floor, Ansari Road,
Darya Ganj, New Delhi-110002
Phones: (Office) 65749511 (Fax) 011-23240261
(Mobile) 9868028838 (Residence) 27562163
E-mail: lakshaythani@hotmail.com

Published by:

SPORTS PUBLICATION
7/26, Ground Floor, Ansari Road, Darya Ganj,
New Delhi-110002
Ph. : (Office) 65749511, 23240261 (Mobile) 9868028838
(Residence) 27562163 (Fax) 011-23240261
E-mail: *lakshaythani@hotmail.com*

I.S.B.N: 978-81-7879-454-9

PRINTED IN INDIA 2016

Laser Typeset by:

JAIN MEDIA GRAPHICS

C-8/77-B, Keshav Puram, Delhi-35

Printed by:

OM SAI PRINTERS AND BINDERS, Delhi

Price: ₹ 95/-

CONTENTS

PREFACE

The present work consists of all ingredients of Snooker Game. It highlights the history, skills and techniques and latest rules of the Snooker Game. It is hoped that this book will prove very handy for the aspirants players, coaches, students of physical education and sports sciences, as well as the general enthusiasts readers.

The whole book is classified into three chapters:

The first chapter deals with the ancient history of the Snooker.

The second chapter highlights all the important and useful skills and techniques of the Snooker Game. In this chapter, all Snooker's skills, tactics, techniques and playing strategies along with their relevant illustrations are described in lucid form.

In the last chapter, all the latest rules of the Snooker Game are described with their court dimension and upgraded version.

Hopefully, the present study will prove very useful for the sportsperson, teachers, students of physical education as well as for the general readers.

—Publisher

1

HISTORY OF SNOOKER

Introduction

Snooker is one of the widely played indoor game in the world, however, it produces a smaller percentage of good players than most others. The actual method of play is very easily grasped. Snooker is played on a billiards table with twenty-two balls, comprising fifteen reds and six colours, namely, yellow, green, brown, blue, pink and black and a white ball. The latter is the only ball that can be struck with the cue. All the scoring is by potting and the mode of play is to pot a red and a colour alternately. Reds stay down once they are potted, but the colours are re-spotted. When all the reds have disappeared the colours are taken in rotation from the yellow and when potted stay down. With the potting of the black, the game ends and the player with the highest score is the winner.

If the players' scores are level at this stage the black is brought back into the play to decide the issue. Thus, there can be no question of a tie. A red counts one point. The colours, each of which has its own spot on the table, are valued in the following manner:

2 points of yellow;

3 points of green;

4 points of brown;

5 points of blue;

6 points of pink; and

7 of black.

Penalties are incurred for going-off, i.e., losing the white and for missing or hitting the wrong ball, and these are to be the value of the ball being played with a minimum of four points. Such points are added to the opponent's score.

It is a much more difficult thing to be able to play the game well, or attain any degree of proficiency. In fact, to become really proficient takes the best part of a lifetime.

It is found that all the present-day professional players started playing the game at the age of 8, 9 or 10 and it is only after years and years of practice and experience that they have become experts. A player cannot reach his peak till he is at least 45 years of age.

Founder of modern game: Joe Davis, played his finest snooker between the ages of 50 and 54. His delayed peak was probably due in some measure to the war when there was a full in competitive play. It is fair to say that the average snooker-player is of novice standard. The percentage of people who advanced from that standard and got higher up the tree is very small.

The essence of any true professional player lies in the fact that he loves the game he plays. No one can approach the top of any sport unless he has genuine love of the game. Only in this way could he put in those necessary arduous hours of practice which are essential for success.

To become a good snooker player one needs many

hours of concentrated practice and an apprenticeship far longer than that of most other careers. Firstly the player should begin on the right lines, if he wants to make progress. Perfect coaching is the essence of a player's bright career. Player should learn to stand properly to hold the cue correctly, to make a firm bridge and develop a correct, smooth cue action.

2

SKILLS AND TECHNIQUES OF SNOOKER

Bridge and Holding the Cue

This is very important as it is the only channel through which the player can guide the cue to make contact with the ball. This is quite a simple thing, yet many players make a poor bridge. They overlook its importance, being content just to place the hand on the table. Too often it is weak and inclined to move.

Importance of the grip on the cloth cannot be overemphasized. It should be so tight that player can lift his any finger with other hand while releasing it would immediately snap back into position on the cloth.

Bridge should be quite immovable and the accuracy of shot will depend on just how well it has been made. The left arm should be extended as straight as possible without creating any strain.

Some people are inclined to bend the left arm a little, but this has the effect of bringing the bridge too close and making everything cramped. So, the player should stretch his arm as far as possible without tension, bridge hand gripping the cloth but with no strain. Player should feel comfortable.

Holding the Cue

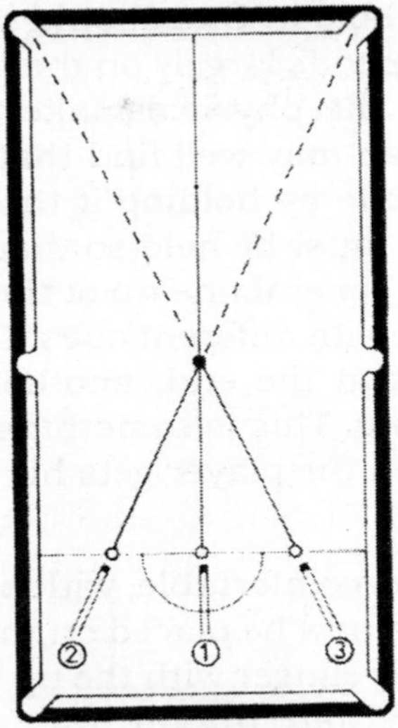

Firstly, the grip is very important. This has always been a controversial subject, and even among good players one will find variation. Some prefer to hold the cue tightly, just gripping the butt with the tips of the fingers; others want to hold it lightly. However, it is generally recommended that the cue should be held firmly. Player should take the cue in the palm of the hand, wrapping the fingers around it. It should be held firmly, but it must not be gripped, because this sets up tension in the arm, a tightness which would restrict the movement. So the player should hold the cue firmly, but loosely enough so that it could easily be pulled out of his hand.

Player should hold the cue in the palm of his hand. If the player is going to knock a nail into the wall, he should not hold the hammer in his finger-tips, for this would give him no control over it. So it is with holding the cue.

A very important question that arises relating to the cue is where to hold it. One should hold it right at the end, but this depends largely on the particular balance of the cue and the physical make-up of the player. Like, a short man may well find that he is better able to balance the cue by holding it three or four inches from the end. It must be held so that it is comfortably balanced in the general line up of the stance, and this will vary slightly with different cues. One cue may need to be held right at the end, another may balance if held further along. This is something that can only be determined when the player gets his particular cue in his hand.

Player should feel comfortable, with perfectly balanced cue. The cue can now be placed on the bridge between the thumb and forefinger with the tip protruding about 6 inches, provided player has followed these instructions closely. His cue should now be under perfect control while travelling freely over the bridge. Now, there should be a direct line through the bridge to the right shoulder with the arm hanging perpendicular over the cue. The elbow must not be cocked in, or out. This should then leave the cue arm to swing freely, and independently, from the elbow without affecting the rigidity of the upper arm and shoulder. This is such a vital position that it is advisable for the player to get a partner continually to check that his forearm is perpendicular and not leaning slightly to the left or right, an alternative option available with the player is to use a mirror in his front.

Stance

It is very difficult to lay down hard and fast rules for

stance, because build and length of limbs vary considerably. But following are some basic principles which are considered to be the essence of stance:

Player should keep his keep at a comfortable distance apart. The left foot should face in the general direction of the shot being played and the right foot should point approximately 70° to the right of that direction. Weight of the body should be on the back foot. Player should move his feet, not the cue to get the right line of the shot. Be slow and meticulous while learning.

Player should keep in his mind that without poise and balance, his success will be very limited. Under no circumstances, the player should allow the right leg to bend at the knee. Very tall player with long legs who finds that he has trouble getting down to the table, particularly when addressing a ball near to the cushion will discover that by spreading his legs very wide and thrusting the bridge arm well forward from the shoulder, he can establish a solid tripod effect style which should suit him.

However, it is important that the feet are spread to take balance, to prevent side sway of the whole body when going through on the shot. This applies to all the players; and the aim is to be solid in style, without being cramped, though many tall men do have rather a problem in this respect.

Use of Rest

Player will need to use the rest many times, and he might dread the thought, particularly if he should be at a vital stage in a game, or in the middle of a nice break at snooker. So, it is as well to learn the correct way to use it right from the start.

In the first place, player should remember that he is

using the rest because he cannot reach the shot in the normal way, so there is little point in using it, if the player is still over-reaching. Make sure you have the right one, whether it be the half butt, the long butt, or normal rest.

While using the normal rest, player should remember that nine times out of ten the butt of the cue is going to be raised far more than would be the case if no rest were used. Since the cue is not going to be parallel to the table, extra care should be taken when the player is striking the ball to avoid any swerving of the ball. Player should follow through nicely, pushing his arm right through the stroke. When using the rest, player's cue arm should be turned to a different position, so that it is moving parallel to the table when making the stroke. Player should use the movement from the elbow to the cue grip in the same way as when playing a normal strike without the rest, but in a completely different manner.

Thus, it can be summarised that unless the player stands correctly, and delivers the stroke correctly, he cannot progress at the game, no matter how many hours he practices. There can be no half-measures; just learn the fundamental of a good stance from the start. Do not just pick up the cue and hit the balls anyhow, by this the player will only regret later. Though, it is far better to have the practical first-hand advice of a coach who can show you exactly what you are doing wrongly.

Flexibility is the key for learning stance, and this can only be achieved by perfect balance. The easier way for explaining the importance of stance for snooker is similar to that for boxing. The same principles apply. Weight must be evenly distributed and the body perfectly poised so that there is no movement on the stroke apart from that of the striking arm. Player should place his feet as if he is going to fight. They should be comfortably apart, the exact distance depending on course, on height of the player. Then, he should bend forward, get his chin well down to the cue.

If the player will do this correctly, his front leg will be slightly bent, while read leg will be straight, acting as a bracer. Weight is evenly distributed, but if anything slightly forward on to the front leg. The forward leg, although bent, must not sag at the knee, otherwise this could lead to a swaying movement. Make sure that the rear leg is ramrod straight, the foot slightly turned outwards but kept firmly on the floor. Point the body in the direction in which the stroke is being made. The whole essence of this position is to make you perfectly balanced and at the same time comfortable.

Common Faults

Player generally commits the following faults while performing the drill:

—Spreading the legs sideways;

—Holding the legs too far apart or too close;

—Bending both knees; and

—Rising on the toes of the back foot.

Selecting a Cue

It is a wrong belief of the people, that professionals use some special kind of cue. There is nothing special about a cue. Any cue is good, provided that the player gets used to it and can play well with it. Player should use the same cue all the time. Importance or value of a cue does not increases or decreases with its worth.

The important thing is to use the same cue all the time so that the player get to know the exact weight and feel of it, and it almost becomes part of him.

If the player frequently changes the cue, then his touch must necessarily suffer. As to the weight of the cue, this varies slightly and is not necessarily of great importance, provided once again that player gets used to it. The average weight of a cue is 16½ to 17 inches. Anything below or above that may still be all right, it is merely a question of individual taste. The standard length of a cue is 4 feet 10½ inches, which all professional players, without exception, find a little too long. They prefer one that is just a little shorter, as this makes it more manageable; a little more compact.

The length of a cue is important. Going to the extremes, it is found to be difficult to play with the half-butt. Nor should the player should use a cue that was only two feet long.

The most important part of a cue is the tip. Player should always see that his cue is of best possible quality and above all he keeps it in good condition. A little care and attention can prevent a lot of miscueing that is often blamed on to the quality of the tip.

Chalking and hitting a hard ball will eventually produce a layer of compressed chalk on top of the tip which leads to miscueing when using side or screw. It is advisable occasionally to remove this hard surface in the following manner:

Take a smooth file and press it over the top of the tip two or three times. Do not file it; just press it over the tip. This will crack off the compressed layer of chalk so that you are once again down to the leather. Under no circumstances use a sandpaper for this purpose as this will cause unnecessary wear. A file is the most suitable tool, but the player should only press it on to the tip, do not file it. Tip wear out and occasionally have to be renewed. This presents another problem.

One gets used to the feel of a particular tip and although its resilience diminishes as it wears, this is so gradual as to be unnoticeable. By the time it reaches the end of its useful life, however, and has to be taken off, the leather has become compressed to such a degree that its feel is by now entirely different from what it was when it was new. So in putting on a new tip the players are faced with the problem of having immediately to get used to a tip with an entirely different feel. This cannot be avoided.

All one can do is to always use the same type of tip to get some measure used to a new tip. For this reason, the player should never dream of changing it before an important match. Players should use a cue that has a brass ferrule at the tip end. This not only prevents the possibility of the cue splitting but is also an invaluable aid to re-tipping. In removing the old tip this thin circle of brass around the edge of the cue ensures that you maintain a perfectly flat surface on which to fix your new tip.

It is quite unnecessary to screw the chalk round and round the tip for minutes on end. Too much chalk is as bad as not enough. Provided your tip is maintained in good condition, a light brushing of the chalk over the tip is sufficient.

Cue Action and Sighting

At this stage, the player is considered ready to swing or perform the cue action. This is effected by the movement of the forearm only. The shoulder must be kept perfectly still, with the forearm swinging to and fro like a pendulum, provided you carry out this movement correctly, the cue should travel backwards and forwards with a piston-like action, which should be short and compact. The cue should not travel more than 4 to 6 inches, but this will vary slightly according to the type of the stroke being made.

Player should keep his wrist supple, so that the cue always moves parallel with the bed of the table. One of the most common faults of cue-swing is to make the movement from the shoulder. This must be avoided at all times. The movement must be made only from the elbow, with the cue travelling parallel to the bed of the table. The stroke should be delivered cleanly and smoothly. It is well worth spending a few weeks doing nothing else but practising swinging the cue so that it becomes instinctively correct. This applies to all sports where an implement designed to strike the ball is used. The implement in this case the cue, must become virtually an extension of the player's right arm. Without this affinity between the snooker player and his cue, he cannot become even a mediocre player, let alone a match-winning.

Perfect Sighting

The sighting of a ball begins just as the player stops walking round the table. He should stand for a second behind the line of the shot, assess the angle and take the stance. He should be able to assess the angle of the shot with enough precision for him to place his feet in the right place. Certain minor adjustments of aim may be necessary, but these should not be enough to involve changing the position of the feet or leaning even fractionally off balance. If either of these become necessary through initial misjudgment of the angle, get up and start again.

People have different ideas of how this sighting should be done. Some never bother to get their heads down at all, but this inevitably means a loss of accuracy. The chin should be down on the cue, so that the player can look right along it. He should not think of firing a rifle when holding it at his waist; he should hold it at eye-level. Same thing should apply to the cue. Player has to get his head right down, so that he can sight along it. Closer he gets to the line of fire, the more accurate his shot is likely to be.

Player should keep his head still, while making the stroke. Player should get into the habit of staying down on the stroke at least until the cue ball strikes the object ball. All movement must be eliminated except for the action of the cue arm. It is a good idea at first to keep the head down till all the balls have come to rest. This will help to eliminate that common fault of jerking up the head at the moment of impact.

There can be no hard and fast rules of sighting. Experts all seem to tackle it in a slightly different way, except for one important fact that is common to all of the players, whatever motions the eyes have gone through while addressing the cue ball, at the moment that the cue tip strikes the white, player's eyes must be focused on the point of contact he desires to make on the object ball. Thus, player should keep his head down.

Potting

To pot is to strike the object ball with the cue ball and knock it into a pocket. This is much more difficult than controlling just one ball. With two balls, there is a double margin of error. Unless player strikes the cue ball accurately, he cannot expect to make the precise contact on the object ball. The part of an object ball that has to be struck in order to pot it is the point of the ball that is farthest away from the pocket.

To find this, the player should draw an imaginary line from the centre of the pocket through the middle of the object ball and where that line emerges is the desired point of contact.

Finding the right angle is very important, but if the player remember the point farthest away from the pocket, he cannot go wrong. The next problem the player faces is to play any of the cue balls into the desired position. This is best achieved by imagining a ball already at the point of contact.

In order to aid sighting of the shot, it is a good idea to place a ball into the position of the imaginary one. Then, get down as if to play shot, carefully noting the area of the red covered by the imaginary ball. After this, the player should take away the intervening, or imaginary, ball and play the shot confidently being careful to strike the cue ball centrally. The last point should emphasize how important it is to master the fundamentals of the game, for until the player has perfected hitting a cue ball centrally, he will not be able to strike the red ball at the correct point.

The easiest post of all should be the one which is perfectly straight. Here the player will be sighting along a straight line of the cue, the cue ball, the object ball and the pocket. There is one thing to remember. The greater the distance between the cue ball and the object ball, and between the object ball and the pocket, the more difficult the shot is. This is because of the distance the balls have to travel.

Most players, when they have been playing a while, can knock in the reasonably easy pot when the cue ball is not too far away from the object ball. But they find that, this becomes increasingly difficult as the distance increases. Greater accuracy is needed.

When the balls are close, the player can sometimes get away with a slight discrepancy. But the greater the distance, the more any slight error is magnified. A clean cue action is what enables the player to produce the necessary accuracy. Stance and cue action are considered the fundamentals of the game, so the player should be perfect in these.

Now, for a few easy pots when the balls are close. Player should place the balls in the correct position. Follow the procedure mentioned above, see that the stance is right, feet comfortably apart with weight evenly distributed, and get chin down on the cue. Player should check the bridge to see that it is rigid; see that his cue arm is hanging perpendicularly and hold the cue firmly, but not tightly. Make a few preliminary waggles with the cue to see that the player has the right action and that he is sighting correctly along the line. Then, he should play his shot. Do not try to force the ball through the back of the pocket. Just hit it with a nice even stroke, striking the ball and following through smoothly with the cue.

Player will not make the pocket at the first attempt, and this may be because he was not sighting the ball properly. In this condition, the player should follow the above mentioned procedure:

Firstly, he should look at the centre point on the cue ball, and line up the cue to be certain that he is aiming at the correct point of contact and that his cue is travelling in a horizontal line. Then, as the cue begins to move, focus the eyes on the point of contact on the object ball. Forget all about the pocket, and just concentrate on the stroke at hand and get a perfect picture of it in the mind.

Player should perform simple pots in the beginning. Each time he trie them, make a thorough check that he is doing everything correctly and soon he will be able to pot the ball with consistency and accuracy.

Once this is achieved, try widening the distance between the balls. Firstly, the player should increase the distance between the cue ball and the object ball and the pocket. He should practice away at these shots, for it is only the practice that leads to perfection. He should not be hesitant on his shot. This can only mean that player is not concentrating properly on the stroke.

Another variant from potting over greater distance is the speed at which the player plays the stroke. He will find it much more difficult to be accurate when playing a shot at speed, since this can so easily produce faults in the cue action. That is why it is so essential that the cue action should not exceed 4 to 6 inches.

Player should keep in his mind that with powerful strokes, it is the forward thrust of the cue which counts, not the back-swing. Keep the cue action short and compact at all times, for it is solely this forward thrust, or follow-through, which determines the power of the stroke. A very important point to remember here is that even with the maximum follow-through at the end of the stroke, the cue must still remain parallel with the bed of the table. In other words, the tip of the cue should follow the path of the cue ball.

Before attempting anything else, the player should make himself sure that he has mastered the techniques of stance, sighting and cue action for the straight pot, and that when making the straight pot, the object ball goes cleanly into the pocket 10 times out of ten. When player can do this, he is getting somewhere and will be ready to tackle the angle shots.

Although, we have assumed straight pot, but generally in the game player does not find himself in this condition. Rarely, he finds balls in a straight line. Player should keep in his mind that point of contact should be always that which is furthest away from the pocket.

One of the big difference between the professional and amateur player is that when a professional makes a mistake, he registers, why, and sees that he does not repeat it. Every player should attempt this. Once the player has found that he can pot the ball with reasonable consistency from the first simple angle, he should look for further variations, by playing the stroke at varying speeds, then by lengthening the distance between the cue ball and the object ball. The greater the distance, the more difficult the shot, as the further the cue ball has to travel before making contact with the object ball, the greater the margin for error.

Positioning around the Black

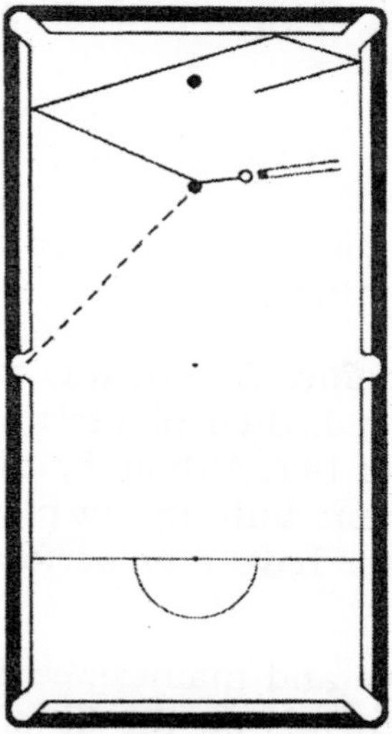

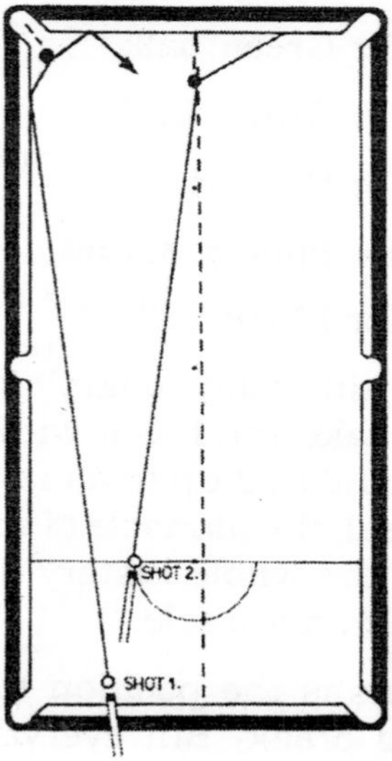

At this stage, the player can make breaks of a reasonable size. Player should keep in his mind that the stance and cue action are the most important skills of all in snooker, and unless he has conquered them, he cannot hope to make progress. Often a player who has a good idea of the game, and who is aiming correctly, still fails to achieve the pot. This is because his cue is not travelling on the correct line. And to get the correct movement, the stance must be just right.

Layout of the table is such that the black, the highest scoring ball, is at the top of the table. It is around this ball that most big breaks are built. Scoring is done by potting a red and a colour, alternately, until all the reds are cleared. After this, all the colours are taken in sequence.

Player should keep in mind the manner in which they count:

2 for Yellow ball;

3 for Green ball;

4 for Brown ball;

5 for Blue ball;

6 for Pink ball; and

7 for Black ball.

Potting black completes the game. The ideal is to try to take the black with every red, then player's score would add up to a maximum of 147. Although, it is an ideal, the pinnacle of achievement, but very few players in the whole history of snooker have ever performed such a miracle.

This is the position to achieve and maintained for a big break. But everything depends on the lie of the reds, and sometimes the player will be forced to come down the table to take other colours in order to keep the break going. Generally, the player must use these colours to lead up the black-ball position. It is the one ball around which there is a close constructive game. Player can keep a break going here as long as there are sufficient reds around, but he will need an extensive repertoire of strokes. Objective of the player should be to make every shot as simple as possible.

Striking the Ball

The essence of all shots in snooker is to be able to strike the cue ball at the dead centre. That is not as simple as it may sound. There is so little margin for error that consistent potting can only be achieved by striking the ball in the right spot. A little deviation to one side or the other and the ball will not run true.

It is not good enough to guess at what spot you think is the centre. You should only learn this by trial and error and the exercise for this is continually to play the ball up and down the table. Player should place the cue ball on the brown spot and play it over the blue, pink and black spots to the top cushion. The object is to get the ball to rebound off the top cushion and run back over those same spots till it returns to the tip of the cue.

Player will not have much trouble in playing up over the spots. It is the return journey that proves the difficulty. It will probably come back wide to the left or to the right of the cue. This is because he has not hit the cue ball exactly in the centre. He has struck it to the left or right, according, that is side-spin, which takes exaggerated effect when it comes off the cushion. A ball that is spinning, cannot run true and at this stage, the player should concerns himself only with plain ball striking.

To return to that up and down the table stroke, this is player's first lesson in striking the cue ball, and till he can do this accurately, he will never make any headway. Player must practice this stroke. With reasonable cure, he should find the central spot to strike about starting to learn. Player should not overlook or skimp this practice.

Every time the player goes to the table, he should play a few of those up and down the middle of the table strokes to get his eye in, and do that even when he has gained a certain amount of proficiency. Clean and accurate striking of the cue ball is the key to successful potting. It is important to remember that the cue ball must be struck with the tip of the cue and not pushed.

Player should remember that the stroke must be cleanly delivered, and the cue must follow through except when playing the stunt stroke. This is the only stroke at snooker where the cue must be stopped suddenly on impact with the cue ball.

At this stage, it is enough to concentrate on achieving an aggressive type of cue action with a good follow-through, remembering at all times that the player's body and head must be kept perfectly still on the stroke.

Screw, Stun and Side

No one has a hope of progressing even to a reasonable league standard without some rudimentary command of the basic spin of the game: stunt, screw and side.

Now, at this stage player is supposed to attain that level by which he can achieve some reasonable control over the plain ball shot and be able to make pots with some consistency, as these will help him to make small breaks, but to make any appreciable advancement he has to learn positional play. A break at snooker is a series of consecutive pots, and to achieve this the cue ball has to be deliberately steered into position for each successive shot, so that the pots are made as simple as possible.

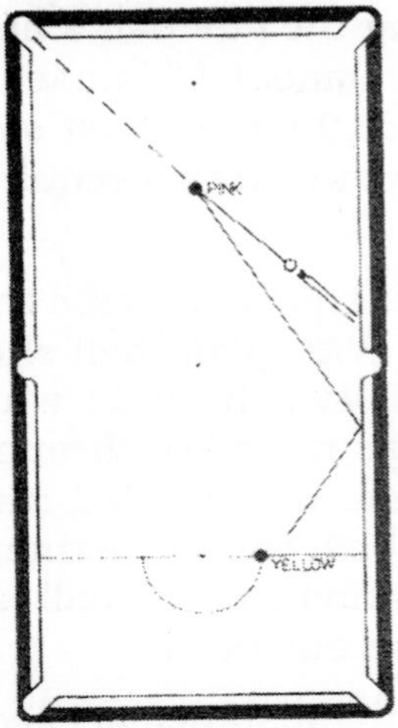

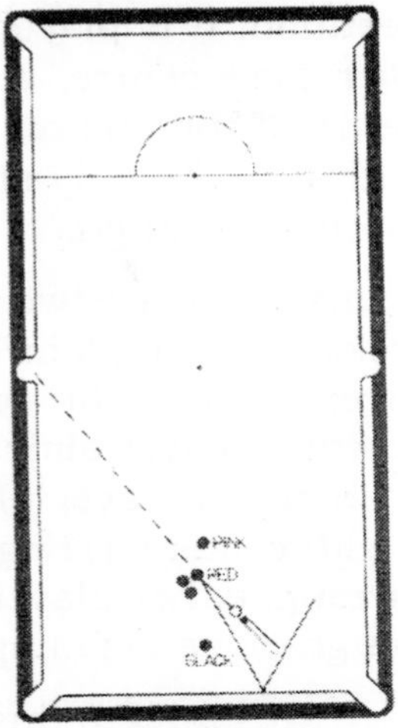

If the cue ball is allowed to run around the table, leaving it to chance where it comes to rest, the player will soon be faced with difficult or impossible positions. Before the player can master this phase of the game, there are two essential strokes to be learnt, the stun and screw. These form the basis of all break-building and about 70 per cent of the strokes played will necessitate their use. Therefore, the player should regard the stun and screw.

Stun Shot

Stun shot is used to stop the cue ball dead. It is used mainly on perfectly straight pots when it is desired to leave the cue ball in the position occupied by the object ball. Many good snooker players find this difficult to master. In fact, it is a difficult stroke to learn. It is a stroke which the player must himself get the feel of, by trial and error. The player should approach it in the right attitude and show no hesitancy in its execution. It is played by striking the cue ball a little lower than centre, and on the moment of impact of the tip of the çue on the cue ball the cue must stop dead. It is the only stroke in snooker which requires no follow-through.

By this, there are two points of difference between this stroke and the plain ball shots. With plain ball shot, player aims at the centre and follow-through; while the stun, player aims low and has no follow-through. If, when the player plays the shot, the cue ball runs on a little after striking the object ball, one of two things is wrong; either player is not striking the cue ball low enough or he is failing to stop the cue dead.

There are limits to this stroke. If the distance between the cue ball and, the object ball is too great then it is impossible for any player but the expert to bring it off. It is mainly used when the balls are from a few inches to 3 or 4 feet apart. The more proficient the cueist, the greater the distance at which he can perform the shot. There are slight variations of stunt, for there are times when player might require the cue ball to run through just a little. This is governed by the point of contact on the cue ball, and by the cue action, but more of that at a later stage.

The place that one chooses to hit on the cue-ball to apply stun varies according to the distance the cue-ball is from the object-ball. If, for example, the two balls are close together, it is possible to strike exactly the centre and still stop the cue-ball running and through.

Before attempting this shot, the player should see that his cue is chalked, however, he should not over-chalk it. While playing stun shot, the player should remember that he should keep himself comfortable, see that his stance is right, and make himself sure that cue is chalked. Then, choose the spot to strike on the cue ball, which should be little lower than the centre; take a short back swing and aim. At the moment of contact, stop the cue dead.

Screw Shot

Screw shots are probably more widely used than any other strokes, and it is essential to master them. Screw can be used to pull the cue ball back for position, or to take it off, at an angle other than the natural one after plain-ball contact. There are usually so many balls on the table, particularly in the top half, that it is impossible to gain a desired position with a plain ball stroke because of cannoning into one of them. Every ball becomes an obstacle which has to be avoided. This is where the screw shot comes in, for it can make positional play easier by enabling the player to thread the cue ball through the gaps. It is played in much the say way as the stunt, with the exception that for the screw, the player must follow through with the cue. Many good players find this difficult simply because they fail to let the cue go through.

Some players apparently have the impression that pulling the cue back quickly after impact helps to draw the cue ball back after it strikes the object ball. This is quite wrong, and must be avoided at all costs. The screw stroke properly executed imparts a backward spin, and the amount of run-back will be governed by the amount of power and follow-through player put into the stroke. The majority of players tend to hit the ball too high, but the player should strike it as low as possible, and to help in this adjust his bridge.

Player should drop the thumb of the bridge hand, and lower the butt of the cue slightly so that the cue is closer to the bed of the table. But, he should make himself sure that travel of his cue is horizontal, otherwise, he can get a lifting action which will cause the cue ball to jump.

It is probably the fear of this, or perhaps or digging into the cloth, that causes so many players to hit high on screw shots and fail to impart the necessary backwards twist. A ball that is propelled by a normal follow-through stroke starts to roll immediately after the initial impact of the tip on the ball. As it rolls, like any moving body, it produces an energy of forward motion. When it strikes a stationary ball, it momentarily suffers a shock from the collision. Its own volition then reasserts itself and ball carries on along its deflected path. With the ball that is played with deep screw applied, however, the ball does not roll with this forward motion, it skids to the object ball, for it is in fact resisting its forward propulsion so that when it strikes the stationary object ball the collision now helps it to assert its desire to spin backwards.

Screw is consider another trial and error stroke. By repeated practice, player will gradually get the feel of it. The essential thing is to remember to follow through. When the cue ball and the object ball are close together, it is sometimes difficult to get the cue out of the way of returning ball. So for practice purpose, it is a good idea to make this stroke with the balls slightly off-straight.

Player should keep in his mind that action for both screw and stun shots should be short and sharp, but he should not snatch at the shot. It must be smooth, just as it is in all other shots. This is where that good stance and cue action proves to be important, as it enables the cue ball to move well-oiled piston.

Achievement of perfection with these two shots is a

matter of feel. Player has to feel the tip of the cue bite into the ball, and he can only learn the strength of this by practice.

Player should remember that the deep screw is impossible when the cue ball is too far away from the object ball. For the amount of rotation, player will apply to the cue ball decreases further it has to run to the object ball.

Side Shot

Player should avoid using side shot whenever possible, but when he is forced into it, there are two things he should keep in his mind. Do not get down to address the cue-ball in the centre and then twist the cue to put the side on. If he do this, his cue will not be driven through a straight line from cue ball to object ball and he will almost certainly make a mess of whatever shot he is attempting. If he intends to put side on, address the cue ball with the degree of side he need right at the start. When using side, grip the cloth firmly with the fingers of bridge hand and make sure that this can be continued till completion of the shot.

All these shots require a lot of practice. Thus, player should not despair. Only by cue-ball control can make the successive shots simple and even the simplest shot can be missed. Player should always keep his eyes open for the stun and screw shots to obtain position, and treat every stroke on its merits.

Breaking Off

In some games, the initial stroke is relatively unimportant since it merely serves to set the game in motion. But this is not so with snooker. Very often a distinct advantage can be gained from a well played break off. After winning the toss in the game, player should not allow his opponent to break off, rather he should use the initial stroke to leave the balls safe, and make the position as difficult as possible for the opponent by trying to bring the cue ball down to the bottom end of the table. If the opponent can be tempted into making a mistake with his first stroke, it may pave the way to a break.

Many games are won on an early break, for it gives the opportunity to take a vital lead. In the professional game, it could start a break of 50 or 60. The ordinary player cannot expect a break of that size from a faulty break-up of the pack, but he can often gain a useful start. It is all part of the strategy of the game. Often, player plays several shots before a red is potted, but the initiative is in the hands of the player who breaks-off.

There are three methods to start the game:

First Method: In first method, cue ball is played on the top cushion with left hand side, so that rebounds into the top of the pack with just sufficient strength to make contact with the reds. This stroke has the advantage of keeping the pack intact, leaving no possible scoring stroke for the opponent. It is somewhat negative stroke, almost as though player was afraid to make the opening gambit. Moreover, it leaves a very simple safety stroke for the next player, who may even effect a snooker behind the black. Player is not making things difficult for him, and this is what your objective should be.

Second Method: This method shows the most common break off used by amateurs. The object here is to bring the cue ball back to the baulk cushion via the top and side cushions, after contact with the corner red of the pack. This is very sound method, as the pack will not be greatly disturbed and the cue ball is left as far as possible from the reds.

The one limitation with this stroke is that all too frequently the cue ball kisses into the yellow or brown on its way back down the table, leaving the opponent with an easily accessible cue ball, instead of being awkwardly placed on the baulk cushion.

Third Method: This method can be termed the Professional Stroke. Although, the objective is still to bring the cue ball back to the baulk end of the table, the path the cue ball takes is vastly different. This is because the shot is played with right-hand side applied to the cue ball. Side causes the ball to come off the top cushion higher up the table and sending it across the table above the blue, and on to the opposite side cushion. From there it again rebounds to the baulk position. This avoids all possibility of kissing the baulk colours. Further, the opponent is left with a most awkward shot from the cushion and the possibility of being snookered behind the green.

Sometimes, the professional will aim at the end red of the second row, still using that running side to alter the angle of throw. Use of this depends on just how much player want to disturb the pack, and that in turn depends on his proficiency and how he feel about the strength of the opposition. If he feel that his opponent is not over-strong when playing from this distance, and that by having broken the pack a little wider, he has a better chance of an early break, then he should try the end red of the second row, by all means.

Player should remember that distance is the big handicap. The target is small, calling for absolute accuracy in cueing. There is also the risk of brushing the end red of the third row which may send cue ball into the top right-hand pocket and cost four penalty points. This is what happens with many ordinary players when they attempt this break off. It is mainly due to inaccurate sighting, which becomes magnified over the distance, or failure to strike the cue ball in the correct spot. To avoid this risk, player should go for the corner red of the triangle, as it is better to be safe than sorry.

In any case, the player still leaves his opponent tied up provided he has played correctly, and the player should remember that everytime he leaves the cue ball on the baulk cushion, he still has the initiative. Always aim to leave the other chap with the awkward shots. Player must fence for the opening to get in with a break, so, he should not rush and keep that initiative.

Snookers

A good general rule for snookering is: if laying a snooker, try to open the balls up; if getting out of a snooker, avoid opening them up.

The laying of snookers, it must be acknowledged, plays a very important part in the tactics of the game. From the beginning to the end of a frame one must always be on the look out for a snooker that is likely to pay dividends, it implies, that very often the well-thought-out snooker may be of greater benefit than an attempt to pot.

In the condition when the balls are arranged in such a manner on the table that green is followed by brown and brown by yellow ball, player should pot a red and leave the cue ball in a reasonable position for potting the brown into the middle pocket. This may well be accomplished, but it would be practically impossible to send the cue ball to the top of the table for the remaining reds in order to keep the break going.

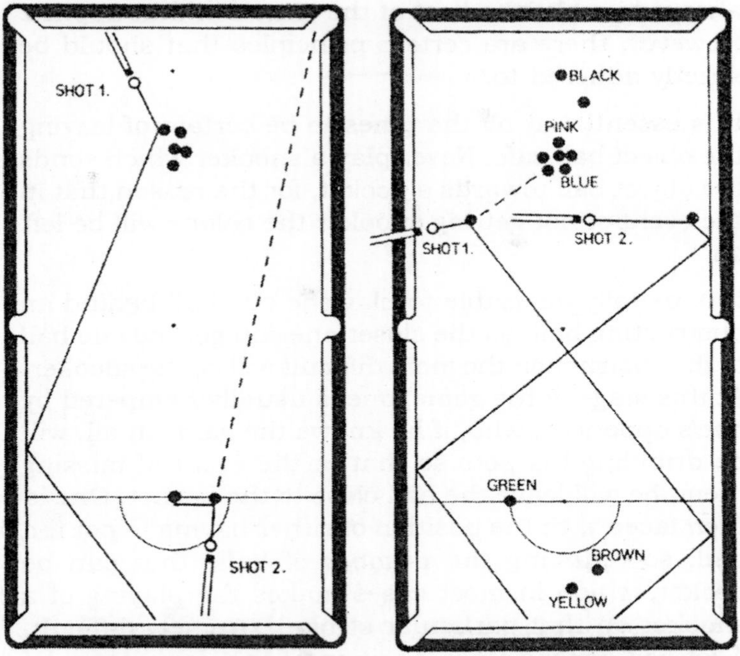

From this position, any player would do well to hit a red, but the important point is that he would be practically certain of leaving a favourable position, whether he in fact made contact with a red or not. It is to force one's opponent into a position where, in endeavouring to hit the ball on, he is likely to leave a favourable position for a break.

Snookers become vital at the end of a game, when only the colours remain, and when one needs to make the opponent forfeit points if one is going to have any chance of winning. A player may be 30 points behind, needing a forfeiture of at least 4 points and all the colours to win. Every game of snooker is different from the one before. There are no set positions, so one has always to make the best of the situation that applies. However, there are certain principles that should be strictly adhered to.

It is essential at all the times to be certain of leaving the object ball safe. Never play a snooker which sends the object ball towards a pocket, for the reason that in the event of not getting snooker the colour will be left on.

It is usually advisable to play the cue ball behind an obstructing ball, as the closer one can get the cue ball to the obstruction the more difficult will be the snooker. At this stage of the game, one is usually hampered by one's opponent, who, if he knows the game at all, will be dribbling his pots so that in the event of missing them, he will leave the ball close to the pocket. One is then faced with the position of either having to pot the ball, so reducing the number of balls that can be pocket, which in most cases makes the playing of a snooker on that particular stroke extremely difficult. A lot will depend upon position of the next colour. If this should be conveniently placed for getting a snooker, it may well be advisable to pot the ball that is over the pocket.

In the situation where last four colours i.e., Black, Pink, Blue and Brown are

left on the table, the player should make strokes in the following manner:

The advantage of getting the cue ball nicely behind an obstructing ball, rather than the object ball. The resulting snooker from stroke I is a comparatively simple one to circumvent via the top cushion, with a little side on the cue ball.

Stroke II, however, when the cue ball is played nicely behind the black, is a much more difficult proposition. It will need to be played off at least two cushions, which, of course, calls for extreme accuracy. In many cases, there will be alternative ways of playing a snooker. Naturally, one should always endeavour to play the one that will result in the most difficult position for the opponent.

Situation in which four balls, Black, Yellow, Pink and Brown rests on left of the table emphasizes the inadvisability of ever playing a snooker while driving the object ball towards a pocket. At first sight the obvious stroke to play appears to be a gentle one on to the yellow, sending it towards the top right pocket whilst nestling the cue ball behind the black. An error of judgment, however, must inevitably result in the yellow being left over the pocket. Even if the stroke were successful the resulting snooker would not be too difficult.

To play the shots efficiently and effectively, player should have a good knowledge of angles. Laying snookers is practically the same as playing cannons.

Looking Ahead

While playing snooker, the player should look ahead. Player should not play any stroke without having first thought about it and formed a plan of campaign. Many ordinary players are content merely to pot a red and a colour, and while they adopt that attitude, they will never be more than ordinary players.

It is very important for the player to plan ahead. A little bit of thought at the beginning often makes the difference between compiling a nice break or merely potting a couple of balls. Many people think that professional players plan a complete break before potting the first red. This is far from true, although we can often see the possibilities of a big break from the lie of the balls. It is essential to be at least two strokes ahead if the game is to be made as easy as possible. Player must decide on the next red before potting the first one.

Positional play is the big secret of break-building and to get those positions you have to plan ahead and control the cue ball. It is no good letting it run wildly, for you will soon be in a hopeless mess. What is more, rigid control and good position can add much to the enjoyment of the game.

Frequently, when going to the table, player is faced with several alternative possibilities. Indeed, it is seldom that you are left with only one possible stroke to play. Usually, you can choose any of the three or four different strokes, and in many cases there are often several different ways of playing the same stroke. The problem, then is which to choose for the best. The answer depends to a large extent on the player. Most of you will have developed your own favourite stroke, a type of shot which you know you can play successfully, and this will obviously have a big influence on your decision.

Break building is a matter of planning ahead. Player has to weigh up the prospects. So do not rush into the first shot that offers itself. Give everything due consideration. While there is often more than one way of playing a particular stroke, it is usually the position of the other balls which help the player to decide on his method of play.

Sometimes, however, there is nothing to prevent the player from playing the stroke as he will. When it becomes a matter of personal choice, the player should choose the shorter and more direct method.

Breaking up the Reds

Making a break at snooker, apart from potting accuracy and obtaining the necessary positions to make the pots fairly simple, depends entirely on the lie of the balls. They are not always conveniently placed for making good positional moves, for the reds may be in unpottable positions. After all, player starts the game with 15 reds and it is obvious from their original placing in the triangle at the top end of the table that they will tend to bunch together, leaving no clear passage to a pocket. This generally happens in the early stages before the pack has been greatly disturbed, but it can happen at any stage of the game, for when only one or two reds are left they might well be awkwardly placed.

At first sight, this would indicate the end of a break and call for a safety stroke. This is the easy way out, but if everyone adopted this attitude there would be very few big breaks. The more expert player will look around for ways and means of forcing an opening. This can often be done by knocking the reds into position when potting a colour. In other words, as the colour is potted the cue ball is made to cannon into the reds in order to split them up.

Often a red will need only a gentle nudge to move it into a more favourable position. Player must get used to looking for these opportunities. At other times, it will call for a much more forceful shot, when, for instance, the reds are tightly bunched, and there are lots of them. In these cases, the player can only hope that as many reds as possible will be favourably displaced, for when several balls are moved it is difficult to judge exactly how they will kiss into each other.

Generally, the player will find that he has forced at

least one opening which will enable him to continue his break. Now, he will emphasise on breaking the large pack of reds. If most of the triangle is still complete, it makes a fairly large target from almost any position on the table. The black, however, when being potted from its spots, offers the easiest opportunity of splitting the pack. According to the position of the cue ball, player can either screw off the black directly into the pack, or, if the pot is at another angle, send the cue ball on to the top at speed in order to displace as many reds as possible.

It is no good playing a soft shot, or you would be bound to leave the cue ball bottled up. The blue can also be used to a good effect for this purpose, but once again it must be played at speed. The path of the cue ball is via the side and top cushions into the top of the pack. It is always advisable to split the pack from the top, as this tends to push the reds down the table slightly, leaving the top area clear for potting the black off its spot. However, there are many different ways of making these pack-splitting cannons, and it is up to the player to study the lie of the balls and appraise the situation before making his decision.

While playing this type of stroke, the player should remember one thing that he should make himself quite sure of potting the colour. It would be a catastrophe to miss the pot and split the reds nicely, leaving it all set up for the opponent. For the beginner, it is not easy to have one's attention divided between potting and positional play. Two-fold shots often lead to failure in one or the other. However, the player has to learn to overcome this if he is to get anywhere, for every stroke in the game, not only breaking up the reds, should have a double purpose. Player has to be able to pot and get position, too, if he wants to make breaks.

Nap of the Cloth

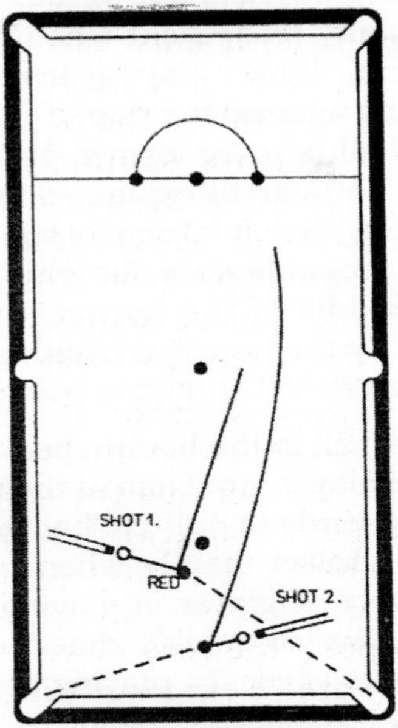

Snooker is not played on wood or formica or glass but on a baize cloth. If one run his hand along the cloth towards the top cushion, he will notice that it feels far smoother than if he does so baulk. This is because of the nap of the cloth.

Bed cloth on which the game is played, plays a very important role in the running of the balls; so some understanding of it is essential. Cloth has a definite pile on it, like that on a carpet or a piece of velvet. This is known as the nap, and is responsible for the marks the fingers of the player's bridge hand make. The nap always runs the same way, from the baulk end to the spot end. Up the table is with the nap whereas down the table is against the nap. It has a definite and consistent effect on the travel of the ball, for which allowance must be made.

To put in an easy way, the nap of the cloth only makes a difference to any real extent when playing down or across the table. When playing towards the baulk, player is playing against the nap of the cloth, and the tendency the ball is to be always pulled towards the side cushions. This can be explained in other way also, if player is potting the pink from its spot into the centre pocket at a reasonable pace, he must always play it not into the middle of the pocket, but towards the bottom bump. By the time it arrives, the nap will have pulled it, so that it will enter the pocket itself.

While playing a ball to the bottom pocket from the top of the table, the player must aim at the bottom cushion jaw, for the nap tends to pull the ball towards the side cushion. This applies mainly when playing the ball reasonably slowly. If player is playing the ball hard, then it is travelling so quickly that the nap does not have time to take effect. In playing across the table, the pull is towards the top cushion.

A few practice shots will enable the player to judge the pull of the nap, which varies from table to table, according to the newness of the cloth. Many a good table have been condemned as out of true merely because of the ignorance of the effect of the nap on the slow-running ball.

Here it is assumed that the player is using his right hand side with the nap, that is away from the baulk. The initial blow which is struck at the right-hand side of the ball will send it out of the left, but the spin quickly corrects this and soon the cue-ball begins to spin to the right. If, however, the player is playing with the right hand side towards the baulk, that is against the nap, the cue ball will not recover from the initial push-out to the left. On the contrary, as long as the side is still in operation, it will curl farther and farther to the left.

Swerve and Potting along the Cushion

A cue action in which cue does not travel parallel to the bed of the table is termed as swerve, a stroke which most players would like to master, as it gives a greater deal of personal satisfaction in its achievement. If one wants to be a useful player, this is a shot he must learn. It can be a most effective reply to a snooker, for instead of sending the ball in a straight line it causes it to describe an arc. Most players tend to think that such a shot is beyond their capabilities, and so avoid it like the plague, yet it is not as difficult as it would appear.

At the moment, player departs from the horizontal path of the cue, he should raise the butt of the cue to an angle of around 45° so that the tip strikes down into the ball, either to the left or right side according to which way he wants the ball to swerve. The big difficulty here for most players is the raising of the butt. It means a higher bridge and player attains this by lifting the heel of the hand off the bed of the table.

Thus, the whole bridge is supported on the finger tips. The tendency is for a wobbly and uncertain bridge, but press firmly with the fingers. The tips of middle two fingers should remain in the same position as if making a normal bridge, but the fore and little fingers move slightly back and therefore give extra support.

The amount of swerve the player places on the ball depends on how high he raise the butt. If he raise it almost vertically the amount of spin applied can be so great that it will cause the ball to complete a semicircle. This is the Masse stroke, more widely used in billiards, but, it can also be useful in snooker.

While dealing with swerve, player should strike the ball downwards with a firm stroke. Feel the tip bite into the ball. The effect of this is to push the ball out until the spin takes its grip on the cloth, which then pulls it back into line. Player should keep a reasonable distance between the cue ball and the intervening ball, and between that ball and the object ball to use this stroke effectively.

A shot that most players hate is the pot along a cushion. Player has faced a situation when a red is resting against a cushion, and, although it is only a foot or so from the pocket, the tendency is to express doubt at being able to pot the ball. It is difficult to pull off because the ball must travel directly along the cushion to the pocket, which from this angle appears only half its normal size. There is only one way to pot this ball. The cue ball must strike both the red and the cushion simultaneously. This and only this will cause the red to roll along the cushion to the pocket. If the red is struck slightly before the cushion, it will bounce off and so miss the pocket.

In same way, if player strike the cushion first then he does not make the correct contact on the red. So, his target must be to hit both the red and the cushion together. Some players find that they achieve more success with this shot at the spot end of the table than they do along the baulk-end cushions. This is due entirely to the effect of the nap. When playing the stroke at the top end of the table the nap will tend to pull the ball towards the top cushion. It is therefore, helpful in keeping in on course.

The reverse applies when player is playing at the baulk end of the table, for he is playing across the nap and the ball is pulled away from the cushion and therefore away from the pocket. Thus, whenever player is faced with this shot at the baulk end of the table, it is advisable to play the stroke a little more firmly so that he give the object ball less time in which to run off.

Player should practice this hot for a while and he will soon learn to sight the stroke correctly and begin to pot it with some consistency. Above all, player should not play it tentatively. Like all strokes at snooker, it needs the utmost confidence.

Plant and use of Side

Plant is a stroke which is of little use for the average player. It is a stroke in which the cue ball is played on to a red which, in turn, knocks another red into a pocket. This sounds extremely complicated but in face is not as difficult as one would imagine. With a little practice, an average player can make much more satisfactory use of the stroke than at present. Player should always look at the lie of the balls and see whether a possible plant is there. The easiest and most obvious of plants is, when two reds are touching each other and are in direct line to a pocket. If the player play as if to pot the first red the second will travel directly into the pocket.

Stroke II is where player can make his own plant, when two balls are an inch or so apart and not absolutely in line with the pocket. It means that the first red must be played on to the second red at the incorrect angle if the second red is to be potted. The best way to determine the angle is to look along the line of the two reds, imagining that the first red is the cue ball. Player must determine the line along which the first red must travel in order to pot the second. Having got this firmly fixed in mind, play the cue ball on to the first red so that it travels along the line, and the second red will be potted. It calls for accurate striking of the first ball, but once player begin to get the idea of this, he will be surprised at the number of times he will make a successful stroke.

Again, stroke III is different and it seems to defy logic. There are two reds touching each other, and not in line with the pocket. They are in line with a point on the side cushion, some two or three inches from the pocket. Player would think to have any chance of making this plant that the first red would have to be struck on the left-hand side, in much the same way as stroke II. This is not so, because the two balls are touching and remember this only applies when they are.

When two balls are touching, the second ball can only be sent along the direct line of the plant if the first ball has been contacted as if to send it along that line. If the first ball is struck to one side or the other of this point a squeeze takes place which causes the second ball to deviate from the line of the plant.

Side is a very complex factor of the game, and needs a great deal of study if its uses are to be fully appreciated. Side is the application of either right- or left-hand spin to the cue ball, and is often used by players without their fully realizing its complications.

Player should keep in his mind that side never helps him to pot a ball. In fact it always make the pot more difficult, so the average player should restrict its use except where it is absolutely necessary. Its main and most useful function is to cause deviations of the cue ball away from the natural path in order to gain a more favourable position for the next stroke. Most players are under the impression that side only takes effect when the ball strikes a cushion, but this is not entirely correct, although it is, then that its effect is most noticeable. Its path on the bed of table is also affected.

With a normal stroke when side is used, cue ball should be pushed out to the right or left, according to which side is applied, and is then brought back on to line as the spin begins to take effect. In other words, it is a swerve in miniature, the curve of the cue ball being less accentuated by virtue of a normal stroke having been played instead of striking down into the cue ball.

The nap of the cloth has its own very definite effect on the ball that is spinning, and this effect varies according to whether the ball is travelling with, against or across the nap. When playing with the nap, that is to say up the table, the cue ball tends to pull constantly in the direction of the side applied. So, a ball played with left-hand side will tend to pull to the left of the straight line, and with right-hand side will pull to the right. When playing down the table, which is, against the nap, player will find that quite the opposite happens. Now the ball carrying left-hand side will tend to pull towards the right, the one with right-hand side towards the left. The amount of this swing varies considerably and will depend upon certain factors:

– speed that the ball is travelling at;

– amount of side that has been applied and;

– the condition of the cloth on which the stroke is played.

The newer cloth will have a much heavier nap than one which is well worn, and a heavier nap will, effect the ball to a far greater extent. To be able to strike an object ball accurately, when all these things have to be taken into account, requires a great deal of study and practice, so that the average player would do well to restrict the use of side at first to the simpler strokes. Side i used in order to steer the cue ball into a more favourable position for the next stroke, but this can be achieved with the use of stun or screw.

Following important points should be kept in mind by the player:

a. Study the swing of the cue ball, whether with or against the nap;

b. Beware the long-range shots, which are far more difficult to judge than the shorter ones;

c. The use of side is purely positional. It always males the pot more difficult;

d. Do not use side unless it is absolutely necessary;

e. Make sure that you do not strike down into the cue ball, as this will inevitable cause a greater swing of the cue ball.

Double

The double is a stroke that the professional players use to a great effect to keep a break going, but which the average player seems either to disregard completely or to approach very tentatively. Make no mistake, this is very valuable stroke to learn, and there is no reason why even the average player cannot bring it well within his scope.

Double implies playing a ball on to the cushion so that it rebounds into a pocket on the opposite side of the table. It is usually a middle pocket, although it can be played into the corner pockets as well. The success of this stroke depends upon the player's knowledge of the angle of rebound from a cushion. As this angle varies according to the speed at which the ball is played, it would be as well to spend some time merely playing a ball on to the cushion at varying speeds and noting the angle of rebound.

Player should avoid the very hard strokes, as a ball played too hard on to the cushion depresses the rubber to such an extent that it is practically impossible for it to rebound at a true angle.

It becomes quite important to describe the true angle here. A ball travelling at reasonable speed will rebound at exactly the same reverse angle as it goes on. In other words, the angle will form a perfect V. This fact must always be the basis of sighting for the double. Only practice can teach the player this, and it is the only by trial and error that you will eventually get the hang of it.

There are various types of doubles, but the main one is the double into the middle pocket when the object ball is reasonably close to the opposite side cushion. It often helps with the sighting of this stroke to stand at the middle pocket concerned and visualize the path of the object ball in reverse, noting the point of contact that has to be made on the cushion. The cue ball has then to be played on to the object ball in order to make it follow this line.

Player should keep in his mind that the corner-pocket doubles are the more risky to attempt. For one thing, the player is playing into a partly closed pocket, and in the event of missing the pot there is the great risk of leaving the ball on for the opponent. This is a stroke which is more recommended to play the cocked hat double into the middle pocket, which gives a greater margin of safety in the event of an unsuccessful stroke. At all times, and even with the double, it is important to ensure that the cue ball is played into a favourable position for the next stroke.

Ideal Pot

Pot into the corner pocket with stun or screw is found

to be the favourite stroke of several snooker players, because of the following reasons:

Firstly, that with a pot that is practically straight, one has the cue ball, object ball and pocket more or less in the line. This is much easier to sight than, for instance, a fine cut.

Secondly, with the balls in this position it is possible to stun or screw the cue ball off at practically any desired angle, which is, of course, an advantage for positioning for the next stroke.

Thirdly, the players feel more confident when playing with stun or screw, as with these strokes one gets the feeling that the cue ball is always held on course. It skids, rather than rolls, to the object ball, and there is no possibility of its rolling off.

Black Complex

It is the tendency among the players to have a go at the higher-valued colours, regardless of the difficulties involved in making the shot, and this happens more often than not with the black. The player becomes so obsessed with the fact that he can score seven points with one stroke that he is oblivious to the existence of the other colours. This is what we call a Black Complex and it should be avoided.

Player should bear in his mind that big things often have small beginnings, and this is particularly true of snooker. First and foremost when potting a red, the player must endeavour to get on a colour and in most instances it should be the easiest colour, not necessarily the one of the highest value. Player must always make his shots as simple as possible. That is the secret of the professional's success. He can bring off many spectacular moves, but it would only be a matter of time being he broke down if his every stroke were an ambitious one. So forget about being black-conscious; go for the shot which serves best from a positional value.

By all means, the player should try to get position around the black, that is the easiest position to work in because of the close proximity of the reds. But use the other colours to get there by easy stages rather than take a risky shot to get at once to the top of the table. Player should plan his breaks ahead from the lie of the table. There will be occasions when, due to circumstances such as an unforeseen kiss, player will not be so favourably placed even though he has potted the red. When this happens, he must scrap the preconceived plan, reappraise the situation and make another plan to suit the new position.

Avoiding the In-Off

Snooker is full of pitfalls. There is nothing more heartbreaking than to go in-off when a game is all on the black. It is noticed that the players pot the back, only to lose the white through not paying sufficient attention to where the cue ball might finish.

Shots which would be a delight at billiards are quite the opposite in snooker. They occur because the ball follows a natural angle into a pocket which the player has not bothered to check. In fact, when player does not want them, those pockets can be just like a magnet. So, the player should make a mental note whenever he gets trapped in this way, and see that he avoids it next time.

Player can make use of some common in-offs in the conditions where black is positioned first on left of the table then red and then blue. They usually occur when playing half-ball shots. Sometimes the player can see the danger there but must still go for his pot. In such cases, he should use a little side or screw to pull the cue ball away and avoid the natural angle. One of the most common of these traps is where the blue is positioned on its spot in the centre of the table and is potted into the middle pocket from a point just below the opposite middle pocket.

Played without stun or screw, this is a natural angle into the top corner pocket. Method of avoiding this disaster must depend entirely upon the position which player desire for his next stroke. That is to say, the average player will be content to merely pot the blue and apply just enough screw or stun to avoid the in-off. But the player who thinks ahead in the game will not only get the pot and avoid the in-off but will also manage to position the cue ball correctly for his next stroke.

Getting out of Snookers

Earlier, we have dealt with laying of snookers, now we are undergoing with ways and means of circumventing them, as snookering is not all one way. Player should know how to get out of them, as well as how to lay them. Escaping snookers is generally a matter of knowing the angles. Some of course, are real teasers, leaving the position completely hopeless. There is usually some way out by using the cushions. It may mean using more than one cushion, to player has to calculate the different angles at which the ball could rebound.

Knowledge of the angles is the first essential, so player should attempt a simple exercise. Drive the cue ball hard from the brown spot on the baulk line to a spot on the top right-hand cushion, about a foot from the pocket, and make a mental note of the angles it takes.

Player should see that when he hits the plain ball, then it should run to true angles. Make variations of this shot from different points. Then try it again with the application of side, to see how that alters the angles. This is all experiment with no other balls on the table, but it can teach the player a lot and is well worth spending some time at.

The single cushion get out should not provide undue difficulty when the distance is not too great, but it is surprising how many ordinary players fail. This may be because they are not aiming at the correct angle, or because they are inadvertently using side. Remember that when playing off a cushion, it is essential to strike the ball as correctly as when potting a ball.

To find the correct angle, the player should stand away from the table, examine and position and look to the point of the cushion which would make a perfect V between the cue ball and the object ball. It may well be that the cue ball and object ball are not in a direct line, so that one side of the V is shorter than the other.

In cases like this, draw an imaginary line through the shorter leg until it does level up. That will give the player his true angle. Having decided this, the player can then move in and play his shot. Another method of playing out of snooker, which is often overlooked by the average player, is by making use of the jaws of the pocket. By playing on to the one side of the jaw the ball will rebound on to the other, then go off along the cushion at almost a right-angle.

In the same way, it is also possible to use the jaw of the middle pocket, though in this case the player uses only one jaw to deflect the ball to the desired degree. Do not use side, and do not play too hard or this can cause the ball to jump. Go for the shot boldly and do not be afraid of going in-off; the pockets are too tight for that, provided that the player hits the centre of the pocket jaw.

Player should remember the number of times he has missed a pot because his ball has boggled in the jaws and he will see little to fear. There is always a comfortable sense of achievement in bringing off this shot, and in most cases, it will leave a look of amazement on opponent's face. It is not a trick shot, just plain use of the angles. The average player is usually content just to get out of a snooker, and will often merely take a bang at the ball more in hope than good judgment. That is the wrong approach.

At all times the player attempts to control the ball and look ahead to see what is likely to happen if he do successfully contact the object ball. Sometimes, there is more than one way out of a snooker. Do not merely take the path which looks the easiest; work out which is the most advantageous. Player should try to leave everything safe. Snookers are not necessarily laid for the penalty points they may gain out for the position they leave afterwards. Many a big breaks have started from the results of a successfully laid snooker.

SAFETY TACTICS

One of the objects of snooker should always be to make the position of the opponent as difficult as possible. This is a phase of the game that is of more concern to the better-class player. The beginner has really very little need to bother himself with safety tactics, for on the

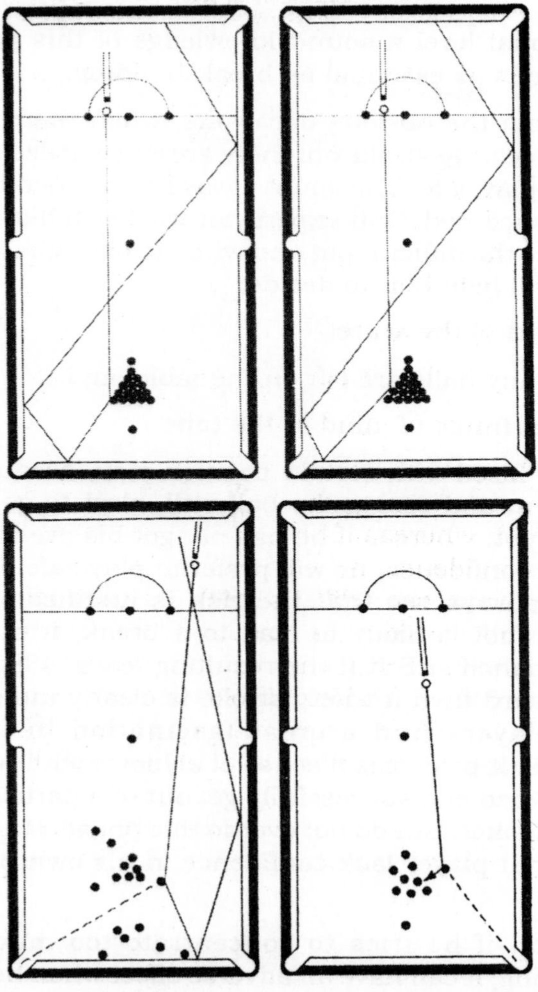

one hand his opponent is unlikely to be of sufficient prowess to warrant making the game more difficult for him, while on the other his own ability is such that he will be unable to take full advantage of any resulting leave. Further one progresses up the ladder, the more important safety tactics become, until at the professional level a sound knowledge of this part of the game is as essential as break-building.

Apart from the obvious occasions, when there is no possible scoring stroke on, there are no set rules about when to play safe. This must always be decided by the player concerned. Only experience will teach him when to chance the difficult pot and when to play safe. Many things will help him to decide:

- The state of the score;
- How many balls are left on the table; and
- His own frame of mind at the time.

A player faced with certain position may, because he is on form and seeing the ball well, elect to go for a difficult pot, whereas if he has not got his eye in, and so lacks confidence, he will prefer to play safe. Player should always see that the risk is justified. If the difficult shot is likely to lead to a break, it may be worth chancing. But if the resulting leave is likely to be awkward then a safety stroke is clearly indicated. Some players find a great fascination in laying snookers. It produces a sense of achievement, just as it does when one successfully get out of a particularly nasty snooker. But do not overdo this phase. It is often a sign that player lack confidence in his own potting ability.

Moreover, if he tries to concentrate too much on snookering, it can have an adverse effect when he does start going for the pots. It is far better to mix potting and safety play, but when to use safety play depends largely on the state of the game, and that the player will learn by experience. So be certain, that it is going to pay dividends. Do not just play safe for the sake of it.

Player should remember that safety play is not necessarily the laying of snookers. It is leaving opponent with nothing on and making things really difficult for him. This can be understood more clearly in the condition when only pink and black remains on the table.

When black lies on its spot and pink on the left side cushion, best safety shot in this condition is to hit the pink full in the face with a very firm stroke, driving it around the table to the baulk cushion.

In case, when pink lies on left side cushion, pink should be played on to the left side cushion so that it rebounds to the opposite cushion. From there it travels to the baulk cushion while the cue ball travels back to the top of the table. Both these strokes may result in a snooker, but in any case the pink will be perfectly safe.

There are other occasions, usually at the beginning of the game, where perhaps only one or two reds have become dislodged from the pack and a difficult pot may be attempted with a modicum of safety in mind. This usually takes the form of a long-range pot into one of the top corner pockets following a safety stroke by the opponent. With this type of shot, it would be foolhardy to attempt a slow pot in order to stay at the top of the table for the pink or black.

Far better in these cases is to play the stroke at sufficient speed to ensure that the cue ball will come down the table to the line of the baulk colours. In the event of potting the red, player will be nicely on one of the lesser colours. On the other hand, if the red is missed a fair degree of safety is ensured by reason of having brought the cue ball well down the table. These are often termed shots to nothing. Make no mistake, for the good player a sound knowledge of safety tactics is most important. He must always be trying to force his opponent into making the mistakes that will create his openings. He must always try to retain the initiative.

Continually leaving the opponent in a difficult position will have a great psychological effect on the player's confidence, and will gradually undermine his morale. Every player will plan his tactics differently, according to his particular temperament. Player should be bold without ever being reckless.

There are two kinds of safety play: aggressive and negative. The first is when without attempting a pot, you actively try to put your opponent in a difficult position. The second is when you merely prevent your opponent from scoring without in any way seizing the initiative which is often just another way of saying that you are giving the initiative away. Take safety shots with the first shot of the frame. Some amateurs, though decreasingly few now, actually start the frame by rolling up to the reds.

Significance of Practice in Snooker

No one, no matter how efficient he is, can expect to maintain consistent form without practice. If one leave off playing for more than a few days, he will feel completely rusty. He must start to miss pots, or find that something is wrong with his positional play and this means that he has to get down to the task of polishing up strokes before he consider playing a match. This is true of all professional players. No one can expect to go to the table whenever he like and bang the balls down as if he has some form of radar control.

Many players think the best method of practice is merely setting the balls up and playing frames of snooker on his own, however it is wrong. There is only one proper way to practise and that is to break the game down into its various components and practice each separately. After all, if player play a frame of snooker, he is not likely to be faced with every type of situation.

Every game of snooker does not follow exactly the same pattern. It is only over a period of games that one can expect to experience all aspects of the game. This is why player must break the game down and practise each phase individually. Spend some time at each till he has achieved consistency.

Whatever reason a player may have for practising, whether it be loss of form, to tune up for an important match or merely the natural desire to improve his game, the method is more or less the same. All players, even the professionals suffer periods of being off form or out of touch, and usually this can be traced to a particular weakness. They are doing something wrongly and their aim must be to discover exactly what this is and then to rectify it.

A professional cannot afford to be off form, and he gets back to the practice table just as often as he can. He cannot wait for a fault to iron itself out on its own. Although, it is possible for faults to rectify themselves without the player knowing why, but this usually takes too long. More often than not these off-form periods are due to a faulty cue action or a discrepancy in the stance. Player may not be standing correctly or he may unconsciously be pulling his head up on the stroke. The missing of an easy pot may be due to over-confidence, or from being so anxious that your action loses its smoothness. Player should make himself sure that he is standing correctly, nicely balanced with feet comfortably apart, weight evenly distributed and the body perfectly poised. He should check that he has no movement on the stroke, except that of the striking arm. Concentrate that he is sighting correctly and keeping the head down; that cue action is smooth with the cue running straight and horizontal to the bed of the table. He should make himself sure that he is following through and not merely jobbing at the ball.

Practice on a Small Table

It is not always possible to reproduce the accurate, exacting conditions of a full-size billiard table in miniature. The proud possessors of a small home table, therefore, will find himself at a disadvantage whenever he plays on the larger table. The angles from the cushions will be different, and some of the spots will be of such long range that the player will feel that he is performing on a ten-acre field.

On the small table, by comparison the balls are bigger, and this, added to the more confined area, tends to create congestion of the balls to such an extent that it becomes extremely difficult to manoeuvre the cue ball into position. There is one aspect of the game that does remain the same. The stance, bridge, holding of the cue and cue action can all be learned just as effectively on the small table as on the full-sized and for this reason the facility of a home table can be of invaluable aid to the beginner.

More on Practice

Although, practice is very important for a snooker player, however, one should not become its slave. It is consider a wrong approach to lay down a practice programme and stick rigidly to it. Practice will only do the player good if he is getting stuck into it accurately, and really concentrating on what he is doing. If player is forcing himself to practice when he is not in the mood, it can do more harm than good. Therefore, it is recommended that player should break off when he get a little tired and do something entirely different.

Importance of Temperament

Temperament plays a big part in snooker, as it does in every other game. It is difficult to define exactly the ideal temperament for this game, and there are conflicting ideas about this. However, player should have the type of temperament whereby he will get annoyed with himself when he is not doing as well as he should. A complacent person, who is playing badly, is likely to accept it with a shrug of his shoulders. The player who gets annoyed with himself, however, will tend to force himself to play better by sheer grit and determination. His very nature will drive him on to greater efforts, making him the player most likely to pull himself together, in moments of crisis, to go on and win.

This event demands calculated concentration, every shot has to be carefully and deliberately thought out before it is played, and the mind must at all times be focused completely on the game, even when one's opponent is in play. The stress and strain that is endured during a closely fought match is terrific. Being subjected to this for such long periods can often make a player over-tense, so that his muscles tighten up to such an extent that he is unable to produce the quality of play to which he is accustomed. At these times, his little show of annoyance, as well as spurring him on to greater efforts, acts also as a safety-valve, allowing him to blow off a little steam, so that he may readjust himself to the necessary degree of tension.

In order to play this game to the best of the ability, one should keep his mind keyed to the extent where all else is excluded, while the body is physically relaxed. This is a difficult state to achieve, as the keying of the mind will often lead to tensing of the muscles. When it is achieved, then and only then, will a player give of his best.

The professional player sets himself an extremely high standard and he is seldom, if ever, satisfied with his performance. His self-criticism is so severe that even when he has acquitted himself brilliantly he will still remember the few strokes that did not quite come off.

Before coming near to table, a player should keep the following important points in his mind:

a. condition your mind to concentrating 100 per cent on the game, whilst being physically relaxed;

b. try to develop a fighting instinct, so that no matter what the odds, given the slightest opportunity, you can always be likely to turn the tables on the opponent;

c. strive for perfection at all times. You would not achieve it, nobody ever has, but it provides the spur that must lead to improvement.

Play in Different Conditions

It is amazing with a game like snooker, always played indoors, with the same sized balls, on the same size tables, and so on, that one can get so much variation in the conditions under which one plays. Two identically made tables may leave the works at exactly the same time and yet when the tables come to be erected they will have small but nevertheless noticeable differences. One of these things which only experience can give is the ability to adjust oneself to different tables.

Though there are some tables which make it impossible for a player to produce anywhere near his true form. The worst thing that can happen is that the pockets can be so tight that it is impossible to pot a ball down a cushion or at speed when one has less than the full face of the pocket to aim at. Tight pockets are only one of the things which can affect a player's play, of course, but they stand out as the only thing they cannot do anything about when they are playing.

Many tables run off, for instance, but player can minimize the effect of this aspect of imperfect playing conditions by not playing any ball slowly when there is any other possible way of playing the shot. Two variable facts which a player has to consider every time he plays are:

a. speed of the table;

b. state of the nap; and

c. quality of the cloth.

A situation in which two reds near the top cushion prevent the player getting position by stunning off the top cushion, shows how the first two factors can determine one's choice of shot. On a slow table with a heavy nap, the correct shot would be to pot the red with a slow screw to hold the cue-ball in position for the black. On a fast table on which the nap has worn thin this might be either impossible or not worth risking. The shot to play in this case would be a screw with right hand side to swing the cue-ball off two cushions. The cue ball is struck with right hand side and rather less screw for this shot. There are many intermediate stages between slow tables with heavy nap and fast tables with very little nap. In each case you have to choose your shot according to the conditions.

Experienced players invariably take all these factors into account unconsciously when selecting their shot. It is well to remember also that two or three centimetres either way can often decide whether a soft screw is on as a means of getting position. What other factors can affect your normal action. Some of them are:

a. If there is too much light in places other than over the table, the limits of the table, particularly the pockets, become less well defined and the spectators and other distractions become all that easier to see.

b. Shots with side are easily missed on any table with a new cloth, especially if it has a noticeable sheen on it through ironing. When one uses, say, right hand side on this type of cloth, the cue-ball pushes out initially much farther to the left before swinging to the right. Thus a shot on normally does not think twice about, like a black off its spot with a touch of side, becomes fraught with danger. A freshly covered table is wonderful to play on once one is used to it, but not so easy if one is used to playing on cloths which are thinner or coarser.

3

RULES OF SNOOKER

TEACH YOURSELF SNOOKER

Introduction

Interpretation of the rules of the snooker leads to more arguments than in most other games. One of the reasons for this is that few people ever read them, and most players tend to base their knowledge on local traditions that have been handed on. The rules are the copyright of the Billiards and Snooker Control Council and their publication is somewhat restricted.

Rules are made to govern the game that is being refereed, where the onus of claiming fouls and stating that must or must not be done rests on a third person. The biggest percentage of games, however, are played without referees and this often leads to complications because there is no one to decide what must happen. Players are advised to have a competent referee whenever you are playing a game of any importance, as his decisions must be strictly adhered to and in this way the game may be played without incident. Certain types of fouls can only be decided upon by a referee.

A player may inadvertently touch a ball with his shirt-sleeve or other part of his body when getting down to his stroke. In most cases, he would be unaware of this and would probably hotly deny doing so if challenged by his opponent, but if fouled by a referee, he must accept it graciously.

Important rules of the game have been discussed below in detail. One should thoroughly go through them before attempting to come near the table.

Game

Description

The game of snooker is played on an English Billiard Table by two persons playing independently or four playing as sides. It is a game of potting and positional play.

Points are awarded for scoring strokes and forfeits from an opponents fouls.

The winner is the player or side making the highest score or to whom the game is awarded.

Each player uses the same WHITE cue ball and there are twenty one object falls- fifteen reds each valued one and six colours :- Yellow valued 2, green 3, brown 4, blue 5 pink 6 and black 7.

Scoring strokes are made by potting reds and colours alternatively until all reds are off the table and then the colours in the ascending order of their value i.e. - yellow through to black.

Position of Balls

At the commencement of each frame the object balls are positioned as follows:

BLACK on the SPOT; PINK on the PYRAMID SPOT; BLUE on the CENTRE SPOT; BROWN on the MIDDLE of the BAULK line; GREEN on the LEFT-HAND and YELLOW on the RIGHT-HAND correct of the "D".

The reds in the form of a triangle, the ball at the apex standing as near to the pink ball as possible, without touching it, the base being parallel with and nearest to the top cushion.

Mode of Play

i. The players shall determine the order of play which must remain unaltered throughout the frame.

ii. The first player shall play from in hand and the frame starts with the first stroke.

iii. A ball not on must not enter a pocket.

iv. The cue-ball:

a. Must not enter a pocket; and

b. Must first hit a ball on.

v. For the first stroke of each turn, until all are off the table, red is the ball on.

vi. If a red is potted, the next ball on is a colour, which if potted is scored. The colour is then re-spotted.

vii. Until all reds are off the table the break is continued by potting reds and colours alternately.

viii. If the striker fails to score the next player plays from where the cue ball comes to rest.

ix. The colours then become on in the ascending order of their value and when potted remain off the table.

x. When only the Black is left the first score or foul ends the frame, unless the scores are then equal, in which case:

a. The Black is spotted.

b. The next player play from in hand, and

c. The next score or foul ends the frame.

d. The players draw lots for choice of playing.

To Play from in Hand

To play from in hand the cue ball must be struck from a position on or within the lines of the "D".

Spotting Colours

i. If a colour has to be spotted, and its own spot is occupied it shall be placed on the highest value spot available.

ii. If there is more than one colour, and their own spots are occupied, the highest value ball takes precedence.

iii. If, in the case of Black and the Pink, the space between its own spot and the nearest part of the top cushion is occupied, the colour shall be placed as near as possible to its own spot on the centre line of the table below that spot.

iv. If all spots are occupied, the colour shall be placed as near as possible to its own spot between that spot and the nearest part of the top cushion.

Hitting two Balls Simultaneously

Two balls, other than two reds or a free ball and the ball on, must not be hit simultaneously be the cue ball.

Penalties

The following are fouls and incur a penalty of four points or the higher one prescribed.

Value of the ball on

By causing

a. The cue-ball to enter a pocket.

b. The cue-ball to miss all object balls.

c. A jump shot.

d. A snooker with free ball.

By striking

a. The cue ball more than once

b. With both feet off the floor.

c. When the balls are not at rest.

d. Out of turn.

e. Improperly from in hand.

—A penalty of seven points is incurred if:

The striker

a. Uses at reds in successive strokes, or

b. After potting a red commits a foul before nominating a colour, or

c. Uses as the cue ball any ball other than white, or

d. Plays at reds in successive strokes.

—Value of the ball on or higher value of the two balls by causing the cue-ball to hit simultaneously two balls other than two reds or a free ball and the ball on.

Fouls

If a foul is committed :

a. Unless awarded by the referee or claimed by the non-striker, before the next stroke is made, it is condoned.

b. All points scored before the foul is awarded or claimed are allowed.

c. The referees shall immediately state FOUL and on completion of the stroke announce the penalty.

d. Any ball improperly spotted shall remain where positioned, except that if off the table it shall be correctly spotted.

e. The next stroke is made from where the cue ball comes to rest.

—The player who committed the foul:

a. Incurs the penalty prescribed, and

b. Has to play again if requested by the next player. Once such a request has been made it cannot be withdrawn.

Officials

The Referee

The referee shall perform the following duties:

a. Be the sole judge of fair and unfair play, and responsible for the proper conduct of the game under these Rules.

b. Intervene if he sees any contravention.

c. Clean a ball on a players request.

d. If a player is colour blind, tell him the colour of a

ball if requested.

He cannot perform the following functions:

a. Give any indication that a player is about to make a foul stroke.

b. Give any advice or opinion on points affecting play.

c. Answer any question not authorised in the Rules.

The Marker

The marker shall keep the score on the marking board and assist the referee in carrying out his duties.

The Players

Non Striker

The non striker shall, when the striker is playing, avoid standing or moving in the line of slight; he should sit or stand at a far distance from the table.

Unfair Conduct

For refusing to continue a frame or for conduct which, in the opinion of the referee is wilfully or persistently unfair a player shall lose the game. He is liable to be disqualified from competitions held under the control of the Billiards and Snooker Council and its Affiliated Associations.

Time Wasting

If the referee considers that a player is taking abnormal amount of time over a stroke, he should be warned that he is liable to be disqualified.

Important Concepts related to Snooker

Game

A game is an agreed number of frames.

Frame

A frame is completed when

(a) Conceded, or

(b) The black is finally potted or fouled.

Match

A match is an agreed number of games.

Stroke

—A stroke is made when the striker strikes the cue-ball with the tip of the cue.

—For the stroke to be a 'Fair-Stroke' the following conditions must be met:

-At the moment of striking, at least one of the strikers feet must be touching the floor.

-The cue ball must be struck and not pushed.

-At the moment of striking, all balls must be at rest, and where necessary, object balls correctly spotted.

-A ball or balls must not be 'forced off the table'.

-The cue ball must not be struck more than once in the same stroke.

-The striker must not touch any ball other than the cue-ball as in section above.

Nominated ball

A nominated ball is the object ball which the striker declares, or indicates to the satisfaction of the referee, he undertakes to hit with the first impact of the cue ball.

Ball on

Any ball which may be lawfully hit by the first impact of the cue ball is said to be on.

Pot

i. A point is when an object ball, after contact with another ball and without any contravention of these rules, enters a pocket.

ii. If a colour, it shall be spotted before the next stroke is made.

Break

i. A break is a number of pots in succession made in any one turn.

ii. If a ball is potted, the same player plays the next stroke.

Foul

A foul is any act in contravention of these rules.

Forced off the table

i. A ball is forced off the table if it comes to rest other than on the bed of the table or in a pocket.

ii. If a colour it shall be spotted. The next stroke is made.

Push Stroke

A push stroke is a foul and is made when the tip of the cue remains in contact with the cue-ball.

i. When the cue ball makes contact with the object ball, or

ii. After the cue ball has commenced its forward motion.

Provided that where the cue ball and an object ball are almost touching, it shall be deemed a fair stroke if the cue ball hits the finest possible edge of the object ball.

Jump Shot

A jump shot is when the cue ball jumps over any ball except when it first strikes the object ball and then jumps over another ball.

Ball moved by other than striker

If a ball, stationary or moving, is disturbed other than by the striker it shall be re-positioned by the referee.

Stalemate

If the referee considers a position of statement is being approached, he should warn the players that if the situation is not altered in a short period of time he will declare the frame null and void. The frame shall be restarted with the same order of play.

Touching ball

If the cue-ball is touching another ball which is, or can be, on, the referee shall state TOUCHING BALL.